this journal belongs to

_____

marie kondo

life-changing magic
a journal

spark joy every day

TEN SPEED PRESS
BERKELEY

Introduction

Once people get into the habit of asking themselves whether something in their lives sparks joy, they naturally start applying this concept to all areas of their lives. By focusing on the things, habits, relationships, activities, and daily practices that truly bring you joy, you can tidy your life of the things that don't. Why waste precious time and attention on things that don't spark joy?

This journal is a space for you to write down what sparks joy for you each day. By taking a moment every day to appreciate the things that spark joy in your life, you will increase happiness and gratitude. If you are looking to make changes to your life, use this journal as a way to envision your ideal life. What would make your job spark joy in you? What about your commute to work? What would make your mealtime spark joy? What about your relationships? The daily errands and tasks that you do?

By imagining actual ways you can spark joy in your life every day, and then appreciating those things and events that do spark joy in you, you will make your life shine.

january 1

20__ _____

_____

_____

_____

_____

_____

20__ _____

_____

_____

_____

_____

_____

20__ _____

_____

_____

_____

_____

_____

Believe what your heart
tells you when you ask,
"Does this spark joy?"
If you act on that intuition,
you will be amazed at
how things will begin to
connect in your life and at
the dramatic changes that
follow. It is as if your life
has been touched by magic.

january 2

20_ _ ⎯⎯⎯⎯⎯⎯⎯⎯⎯⎯⎯⎯⎯⎯⎯⎯⎯⎯⎯⎯
⎯⎯⎯⎯⎯⎯⎯⎯⎯⎯⎯⎯⎯⎯⎯⎯⎯⎯⎯⎯⎯⎯⎯⎯
⎯⎯⎯⎯⎯⎯⎯⎯⎯⎯⎯⎯⎯⎯⎯⎯⎯⎯⎯⎯⎯⎯⎯⎯
⎯⎯⎯⎯⎯⎯⎯⎯⎯⎯⎯⎯⎯⎯⎯⎯⎯⎯⎯⎯⎯⎯⎯⎯
⎯⎯⎯⎯⎯⎯⎯⎯⎯⎯⎯⎯⎯⎯⎯⎯⎯⎯⎯⎯⎯⎯⎯⎯
⎯⎯⎯⎯⎯⎯⎯⎯⎯⎯⎯⎯⎯⎯⎯⎯⎯⎯⎯⎯⎯⎯⎯⎯

20_ _ ⎯⎯⎯⎯⎯⎯⎯⎯⎯⎯⎯⎯⎯⎯⎯⎯⎯⎯⎯⎯
⎯⎯⎯⎯⎯⎯⎯⎯⎯⎯⎯⎯⎯⎯⎯⎯⎯⎯⎯⎯⎯⎯⎯⎯
⎯⎯⎯⎯⎯⎯⎯⎯⎯⎯⎯⎯⎯⎯⎯⎯⎯⎯⎯⎯⎯⎯⎯⎯
⎯⎯⎯⎯⎯⎯⎯⎯⎯⎯⎯⎯⎯⎯⎯⎯⎯⎯⎯⎯⎯⎯⎯⎯
⎯⎯⎯⎯⎯⎯⎯⎯⎯⎯⎯⎯⎯⎯⎯⎯⎯⎯⎯⎯⎯⎯⎯⎯
⎯⎯⎯⎯⎯⎯⎯⎯⎯⎯⎯⎯⎯⎯⎯⎯⎯⎯⎯⎯⎯⎯⎯⎯

20_ _ ⎯⎯⎯⎯⎯⎯⎯⎯⎯⎯⎯⎯⎯⎯⎯⎯⎯⎯⎯⎯
⎯⎯⎯⎯⎯⎯⎯⎯⎯⎯⎯⎯⎯⎯⎯⎯⎯⎯⎯⎯⎯⎯⎯⎯
⎯⎯⎯⎯⎯⎯⎯⎯⎯⎯⎯⎯⎯⎯⎯⎯⎯⎯⎯⎯⎯⎯⎯⎯
⎯⎯⎯⎯⎯⎯⎯⎯⎯⎯⎯⎯⎯⎯⎯⎯⎯⎯⎯⎯⎯⎯⎯⎯
⎯⎯⎯⎯⎯⎯⎯⎯⎯⎯⎯⎯⎯⎯⎯⎯⎯⎯⎯⎯⎯⎯⎯⎯
⎯⎯⎯⎯⎯⎯⎯⎯⎯⎯⎯⎯⎯⎯⎯⎯⎯⎯⎯⎯⎯⎯⎯⎯

january 3

Does it spark joy?

20__ _____

_____

_____

_____

_____

20__ _____

_____

_____

_____

_____

20__ _____

_____

_____

_____

_____

january 4

20_ _ _____
_____
_____
_____
_____
_____

20_ _ _____
_____
_____
_____
_____
_____

20_ _ _____
_____
_____
_____
_____
_____

january 5

20_ _ _____

_____

_____

_____

_____

_____

20_ _ _____

_____

_____

_____

_____

_____

20_ _ _____

_____

_____

_____

_____

_____

january 6

20_ _ _____

_____

_____

_____

_____

_____

20_ _ _____

_____

_____

_____

_____

_____

20_ _ _____

_____

_____

_____

_____

_____

january 7

Does it spark joy?

20_ _ _____

_____

_____

_____

_____

_____

20_ _ _____

_____

_____

_____

_____

_____

20_ _ _____

_____

_____

_____

_____

_____

january 8

20_ _ _____

_____

_____

_____

_____

_____

20_ _ _____

_____

_____

_____

_____

_____

20_ _ _____

_____

_____

_____

_____

_____

january 9

20_ _ _____

_____

_____

_____

_____

_____

20_ _ _____

_____

_____

_____

_____

_____

20_ _ _____

_____

_____

_____

_____

_____

january 10

20_ _ _____

20_ _ _____

20_ _ _____

january 11

Does it spark joy?

20_ _ _____
_____
_____
_____
_____
_____

20_ _ _____
_____
_____
_____
_____
_____

20_ _ _____
_____
_____
_____
_____
_____

Pour your time and passion into what brings you the most joy, your mission in life.

january 12

20_ _ _____

20_ _ _____

20_ _ _____

january 13

20_ _ _____

_____

_____

_____

_____

_____

20_ _ _____

_____

_____

_____

_____

_____

20_ _ _____

_____

_____

_____

_____

_____

january 14

Does it spark joy?

20_ _ _____

_____

_____

_____

_____

20_ _ _____

_____

_____

_____

_____

20_ _ _____

_____

_____

_____

_____

january 15

20_ _ _____

_____

_____

_____

_____

_____

20_ _ _____

_____

_____

_____

_____

_____

20_ _ _____

_____

_____

_____

_____

_____

january 16

20_ _ _____

_____

_____

_____

_____

_____

20_ _ _____

_____

_____

_____

_____

_____

20_ _ _____

_____

_____

_____

_____

_____

january 17

20_ _ _____

_____

_____

_____

_____

_____

20_ _ _____

_____

_____

_____

_____

_____

20_ _ _____

_____

_____

_____

_____

_____

january 18

Does it spark joy?

20_ _ —————————————————————————
_____
_____
_____
_____
_____

20_ _ —————————————————————————
_____
_____
_____
_____
_____

20_ _ —————————————————————————
_____
_____
_____
_____
_____

january 19

20_ _ _____

_____

_____

_____

_____

_____

20_ _ _____

_____

_____

_____

_____

_____

20_ _ _____

_____

_____

_____

_____

_____

january 20

20_ _ _____

_____

_____

_____

_____

_____

20_ _ _____

_____

_____

_____

_____

20_ _ _____

_____

_____

_____

_____

january 21

20_ _ _____

_____

_____

_____

_____

_____

20_ _ _____

_____

_____

_____

_____

_____

20_ _ _____

_____

_____

_____

_____

_____

january 22

Does it spark joy?

20___ _____

_____

_____

_____

_____

20___ _____

_____

_____

_____

_____

20___ _____

_____

_____

_____

_____

january 23

20_ _ _____

20_ _ _____

20_ _ _____

Before you start, visualize your destination.

january 24

20_ _ _____

_____

_____

_____

_____

_____

20_ _ _____

_____

_____

_____

_____

_____

20_ _ _____

_____

_____

_____

_____

_____

january 25

Does it spark joy?

20___ _____

_____

_____

_____

_____

20___ _____

_____

_____

_____

_____

20___ _____

_____

_____

_____

_____

january 26

20_ _ _____

20_ _ _____

20_ _ _____

january 27

20__ _____

_____

_____

_____

_____

_____

20__ _____

_____

_____

_____

_____

_____

20__ _____

_____

_____

_____

_____

_____

january 28

20_ _ _____

_____

_____

_____

_____

_____

20_ _ _____

_____

_____

_____

_____

_____

20_ _ _____

_____

_____

_____

_____

_____

january 29

Does it spark joy?

20_ _ _____

_____

_____

_____

_____

20_ _ _____

_____

_____

_____

_____

20_ _ _____

_____

_____

_____

_____

january 30

20__ _____

_____

_____

_____

_____

20__ _____

_____

_____

_____

_____

20__ _____

_____

_____

_____

_____

january 31

20_ _ _____
_____
_____
_____
_____
_____

20_ _ _____
_____
_____
_____
_____
_____

20_ _ _____
_____
_____
_____
_____
_____

february 1

20__ _____
_____
_____
_____
_____

20__ _____
_____
_____
_____
_____

20__ _____
_____
_____
_____
_____

february 2

Does it spark joy?

20＿＿

_____

20＿＿

_____

20＿＿

_____

february 3

20_ _ _____

_____

_____

_____

_____

_____

20_ _ _____

_____

_____

_____

_____

_____

20_ _ _____

_____

_____

_____

_____

_____

february 4

20__ _____

_____

_____

_____

_____

20__ _____

_____

_____

_____

_____

20__ _____

_____

_____

_____

_____

Follow your intuition
and all will be well.

february 5

20_ _ _____

_____

_____

_____

_____

_____

20_ _ _____

_____

_____

_____

_____

_____

20_ _ _____

_____

_____

_____

_____

_____

february 6

20_ _   _____

_____

_____

_____

_____

_____

20_ _   _____

_____

_____

_____

_____

_____

20_ _   _____

_____

_____

_____

_____

_____

february 7

20___ _____

_____

_____

_____

_____

20___ _____

_____

_____

_____

_____

20___ _____

_____

_____

_____

_____

february 8

20__ _____

_____

_____

_____

_____

_____

20__ _____

_____

_____

_____

_____

_____

20__ _____

_____

_____

_____

_____

_____

february 9

20_ _ _____

_____

_____

_____

_____

_____

20_ _ _____

_____

_____

_____

_____

_____

20_ _ _____

_____

_____

_____

_____

_____

february 10

20_ _ _____

_____

_____

_____

_____

_____

20_ _ _____

_____

_____

_____

_____

_____

20_ _ _____

_____

_____

_____

_____

_____

february 11

20___ _____

_____

_____

_____

_____

_____

20___ _____

_____

_____

_____

_____

_____

20___ _____

_____

_____

_____

_____

_____

february 12

20_ _ _____

_____

_____

_____

_____

_____

20_ _ _____

_____

_____

_____

_____

_____

20_ _ _____

_____

_____

_____

_____

_____

february 13

20_ _ _____

_____

_____

_____

_____

_____

20_ _ _____

_____

_____

_____

_____

_____

20_ _ _____

_____

_____

_____

_____

_____

february 14

20_ _ _____

_____

_____

_____

_____

_____

20_ _ _____

_____

_____

_____

_____

_____

20_ _ _____

_____

_____

_____

_____

_____

february 15

20__ __ _____

_____

_____

_____

_____

_____

20__ __ _____

_____

_____

_____

_____

_____

20__ __ _____

_____

_____

_____

_____

_____

february 16

0___ ___

20___ ___

20___ ___

Pursue ultimate simplicity.

february 17

20_ _ _____

_____

_____

_____

_____

20_ _ _____

_____

_____

_____

_____

20_ _ _____

_____

_____

_____

_____

february 18

Does it spark joy?

20__ _____

_____

_____

_____

_____

20__ _____

_____

_____

_____

_____

20__ _____

_____

_____

_____

_____

february 19

20__ _____

_____

_____

_____

_____

_____

20__ _____

_____

_____

_____

_____

_____

20__ _____

_____

_____

_____

_____

_____

february 20

20_ _ _____

_____

_____

_____

_____

_____

20_ _ _____

_____

_____

_____

_____

_____

20_ _ _____

_____

_____

_____

_____

_____

february 21

20_ _ _____

_____

_____

_____

_____

20_ _ _____

_____

_____

_____

_____

20_ _ _____

_____

_____

_____

_____

february 22

Does it spark joy?

20___ _____

_____

_____

_____

_____

_____

20___ _____

_____

_____

_____

_____

_____

20___ _____

_____

_____

_____

_____

_____

february 23

20_ _ _____

_____

_____

_____

_____

_____

20_ _ _____

_____

_____

_____

_____

_____

20_ _ _____

_____

_____

_____

_____

_____

february 24

20__ _____

_____

_____

_____

_____

_____

20__ _____

_____

_____

_____

_____

_____

20__ _____

_____

_____

_____

_____

_____

february 25

20__ _____

_____

_____

_____

_____

_____

20__ _____

_____

_____

_____

_____

_____

20__ _____

_____

_____

_____

_____

_____

february 26

Does it spark joy?

20___ _____

_____

_____

_____

_____

20___ _____

_____

_____

_____

_____

20___ _____

_____

_____

_____

_____

Make your life shine.

february 27

20__ __ _____

_____

_____

_____

_____

20__ __ _____

_____

_____

_____

_____

20__ __ _____

_____

_____

_____

_____

february 28

20_ _ _____

_____

_____

_____

_____

_____

20_ _ _____

_____

_____

_____

_____

_____

20_ _ _____

_____

_____

_____

_____

_____

february 29

20_ _ _____

_____

_____

_____

_____

_____

20_ _ _____

_____

_____

_____

_____

_____

20_ _ _____

_____

_____

_____

_____

_____

march 1

20_ _ _____

_____

_____

_____

_____

_____

20_ _ _____

_____

_____

_____

_____

_____

20_ _ _____

_____

_____

_____

_____

_____

march 2

Does it spark joy?

20_ _ _ _____

_____

_____

_____

_____

20_ _ _ _____

_____

_____

_____

_____

20_ _ _ _____

_____

_____

_____

_____

march 3

20_ _ _____

_____

_____

_____

_____

_____

20_ _ _____

_____

_____

_____

_____

_____

20_ _ _____

_____

_____

_____

_____

_____

march 4

20＿＿

20＿＿

20＿＿

march 5

20_ _ _____

_____

_____

_____

_____

_____

20_ _ _____

_____

_____

_____

_____

20_ _ _____

_____

_____

_____

_____

_____

march 6

20_ _ _____

_____

_____

_____

_____

_____

20_ _ _____

_____

_____

_____

_____

20_ _ _____

_____

_____

_____

_____

march 7

20_ _ _____

_____

_____

_____

_____

_____

20_ _ _____

_____

_____

_____

_____

_____

20_ _ _____

_____

_____

_____

_____

_____

march 8

20_ _ _____

_____

_____

_____

_____

_____

20_ _ _____

_____

_____

_____

_____

_____

20_ _ _____

_____

_____

_____

_____

_____

march 9

20_ _ _____

_____

_____

_____

_____

_____

20_ _ _____

_____

_____

_____

_____

_____

20_ _ _____

_____

_____

_____

_____

_____

march **10**

Does it spark joy?

20_ _ _____

_____

_____

_____

_____

_____

20_ _ _____

_____

_____

_____

_____

20_ _ _____

_____

_____

_____

_____

march 11

20_ _ _____

_____

_____

_____

_____

_____

20_ _ _____

_____

_____

_____

_____

_____

20_ _ _____

_____

_____

_____

_____

_____

Identify what is truly
precious.

20_ _ _____

_____

_____

_____

_____

_____

20_ _ _____

_____

_____

_____

_____

_____

20_ _ _____

_____

_____

_____

_____

_____

march 13

Does it spark joy?

20___ _____

_____

_____

_____

_____

20___ _____

_____

_____

_____

_____

20___ _____

_____

_____

_____

_____

march 14

20_ _ _____

_____

_____

_____

_____

_____

20_ _ _____

_____

_____

_____

_____

_____

20_ _ _____

_____

_____

_____

_____

_____

march 15

20＿＿

_____

_____

_____

_____

_____

20＿＿

_____

_____

_____

_____

_____

20＿＿

_____

_____

_____

_____

_____

march 16

20_ _ _ _____

20_ _ _ _____

20_ _ _ _____

march 17

Does it spark joy?

20_ _ _____

_____

_____

_____

_____

20_ _ _____

_____

_____

_____

_____

20_ _ _____

_____

_____

_____

_____

march 18

20_ _ _____

20_ _ _____

20_ _ _____

march 19

20_ _ _____

_____

_____

_____

_____

_____

20_ _ _____

_____

_____

_____

_____

_____

20_ _ _____

_____

_____

_____

_____

_____

march 20

20_ _ _____

_____

_____

_____

_____

_____

20_ _ _____

_____

_____

_____

_____

_____

20_ _ _____

_____

_____

_____

_____

_____

march **21**

20 _ _ _____

_____

_____

_____

_____

_____

20 _ _ _____

_____

_____

_____

_____

_____

20 _ _ _____

_____

_____

_____

_____

_____

march 22

20_ _ _____
_____
_____
_____
_____
_____

20_ _ _____
_____
_____
_____
_____
_____

20_ _ _____
_____
_____
_____
_____
_____

march 23

20_ _ _____

_____

_____

_____

_____

20_ _ _____

_____

_____

_____

_____

20_ _ _____

_____

_____

_____

_____

march 24

20_ _ _____

_____

_____

_____

_____

_____

20_ _ _____

_____

_____

_____

_____

_____

20_ _ _____

_____

_____

_____

_____

_____

march **25**

20_ _ _____

_____

_____

_____

_____

20_ _ _____

_____

_____

_____

_____

20_ _ _____

_____

_____

_____

_____

Being surrounded
by things that spark joy
makes you happy.

march 26

20___ _____

_____

_____

_____

_____

20___ _____

_____

_____

_____

_____

20___ _____

_____

_____

_____

_____

march 27

20_ _ _____

_____

_____

_____

_____

_____

20_ _ _____

_____

_____

_____

_____

_____

20_ _ _____

_____

_____

_____

_____

_____

Does it spark joy?

20_ _ _____

_____

_____

_____

_____

_____

20_ _ _____

_____

_____

_____

_____

_____

20_ _ _____

_____

_____

_____

_____

_____

march 29

20_ _ _____

_____

_____

_____

_____

20_ _ _____

_____

_____

_____

_____

20_ _ _____

_____

_____

_____

_____

march 30

20__ _____

_____

_____

_____

_____

_____

20__ _____

_____

_____

_____

_____

_____

20__ _____

_____

_____

_____

_____

_____

march **31**

20_ _ _____

_____
_____
_____
_____
_____

20_ _ _____

_____
_____
_____
_____
_____

20_ _ _____

_____
_____
_____
_____
_____

april 1

Does it spark joy?

20＿＿ _____

_____

_____

_____

_____

20＿＿ _____

_____

_____

_____

_____

20＿＿ _____

_____

_____

_____

_____

april 2

20_ _ _____

_____

_____

_____

_____

_____

20_ _ _____

_____

_____

_____

_____

_____

20_ _ _____

_____

_____

_____

_____

_____

april 3

20_ _

20_ _

20_ _

april 4

20__ _____

_____

_____

_____

_____

_____

20__ _____

_____

_____

_____

_____

_____

20__ _____

_____

_____

_____

_____

_____

april 5

20＿＿ _____

_____

_____

_____

_____

_____

20＿＿ _____

_____

_____

_____

_____

_____

20＿＿ _____

_____

_____

_____

_____

april 6

20___ _____
_____
_____
_____
_____
_____

20___ _____
_____
_____
_____
_____
_____

20___ _____
_____
_____
_____
_____
_____

People cannot change
their habits without
first changing their way
of thinking.

april 7

20_ _ _____

_____

_____

_____

_____

_____

20_ _ _____

_____

_____

_____

_____

_____

20_ _ _____

_____

_____

_____

_____

_____

april 8

20___ _____

_____

_____

_____

_____

_____

20___ _____

_____

_____

_____

_____

_____

20___ _____

_____

_____

_____

_____

_____

april 9

20___ _____
_____
_____
_____
_____
_____

20___ _____
_____
_____
_____
_____
_____

20___ _____
_____
_____
_____
_____
_____

april 10

20_ _ _____

_____

_____

_____

_____

20_ _ _____

_____

_____

_____

_____

20_ _ _____

_____

_____

_____

_____

april 11

20_ _ _____

_____

_____

_____

_____

_____

20_ _ _____

_____

_____

_____

_____

_____

20_ _ _____

_____

_____

_____

_____

_____

april 12

Does it spark joy?

20_ _ —————————————————————

———————————————————————————————

———————————————————————————————

———————————————————————————————

———————————————————————————————

———————————————————————————————

20_ _ —————————————————————

———————————————————————————————

———————————————————————————————

———————————————————————————————

———————————————————————————————

———————————————————————————————

20_ _ —————————————————————

———————————————————————————————

———————————————————————————————

———————————————————————————————

———————————————————————————————

———————————————————————————————

^{april} 13

20_ _ _____

_____

_____

_____

_____

20_ _ _____

_____

_____

_____

_____

20_ _ _____

_____

_____

_____

_____

april 14

20_ _ _____

_____

_____

_____

_____

_____

20_ _ _____

_____

_____

_____

_____

_____

20_ _ _____

_____

_____

_____

_____

_____

april 15

20_ _ _____
_____
_____
_____
_____
_____

20_ _ _____
_____
_____
_____
_____
_____

20_ _ _____
_____
_____
_____
_____
_____

april **16**

Does it spark joy?

20＿＿ _____

_____

_____

_____

_____

_____

20＿＿ _____

_____

_____

_____

_____

_____

20＿＿ _____

_____

_____

_____

_____

_____

20__ _____

_____

_____

_____

_____

_____

20__ _____

_____

_____

_____

_____

_____

20__ _____

_____

_____

_____

_____

_____

april 18

20_ _ _____

_____

_____

_____

_____

_____

20_ _ _____

_____

_____

_____

_____

_____

20_ _ _____

_____

_____

_____

_____

_____

If you let the temporary relief achieved by tidying up your physical space deceive you, you will never recognize the need to clean up your psychological space.

april 19

20_ _ _____

_____
_____
_____
_____
_____

20_ _ _____

_____
_____
_____
_____
_____

20_ _ _____

_____
_____
_____
_____
_____

april 20

20__ _____

_____

_____

_____

_____

_____

20__ _____

_____

_____

_____

_____

_____

20__ _____

_____

_____

_____

_____

april 21

Does it spark joy?

20_ _ _____

_____

_____

_____

_____

_____

20_ _ _____

_____

_____

_____

_____

_____

20_ _ _____

_____

_____

_____

_____

_____

april 22

20_ _ _____

_____

_____

_____

_____

_____

20_ _ _____

_____

_____

_____

_____

_____

20_ _ _____

_____

_____

_____

_____

_____

april 23

20_ _ _____

_____

_____

_____

_____

20_ _ _____

_____

_____

_____

_____

20_ _ _____

_____

_____

_____

_____

april 24

20___ _____

_____

_____

_____

_____

20___ _____

_____

_____

_____

_____

20___ _____

_____

_____

_____

_____

april 25

Does it spark joy?

20_ _ _____

_____

_____

_____

_____

20_ _ _____

_____

_____

_____

_____

20_ _ _____

_____

_____

_____

_____

april 26

20_ _ _____
_____
_____
_____
_____
_____

20_ _ _____
_____
_____
_____
_____
_____

20_ _ _____
_____
_____
_____
_____
_____

^{april} 27

20_ _

20_ _

20_ _

april 28

20_ _ _____

_____

_____

_____

_____

20_ _ _____

_____

_____

_____

_____

20_ _ _____

_____

_____

_____

_____

april **29**

Does it spark joy?

20_ _ _____

_____

_____

_____

_____

_____

20_ _ _____

_____

_____

_____

_____

_____

20_ _ _____

_____

_____

_____

_____

_____

april 30

20_ _ —————————————————————————
————————————————————————————————
————————————————————————————————
————————————————————————————————
————————————————————————————————
————————————————————————————————

20_ _ —————————————————————————
————————————————————————————————
————————————————————————————————
————————————————————————————————
————————————————————————————————
————————————————————————————————

20_ _ —————————————————————————
————————————————————————————————
————————————————————————————————
————————————————————————————————
————————————————————————————————
————————————————————————————————

If we can have confidence
in our decisions and
launch enthusiastically
into action without any
doubts holding us back,
we will be able to achieve
much more.

may 1

20_ _ _____

_____

_____

_____

_____

20_ _ _____

_____

_____

_____

_____

20_ _ _____

_____

_____

_____

_____

_____

may 2

20_ _ _____

_____

_____

_____

_____

_____

20_ _ _____

_____

_____

_____

_____

_____

20_ _ _____

_____

_____

_____

_____

_____

may 3

20_ _ _____
_____
_____
_____
_____
_____

20_ _ _____
_____
_____
_____
_____
_____

20_ _ _____
_____
_____
_____
_____
_____

20_ _

20_ _

20_ _

may 5

20_ _ _____

_____

_____

_____

_____

_____

20_ _ _____

_____

_____

_____

_____

_____

20_ _ _____

_____

_____

_____

_____

_____

may 6

Does it spark joy?

20_ _ _____

_____

_____

_____

_____

20_ _ _____

_____

_____

_____

_____

20_ _ _____

_____

_____

_____

_____

may 7

20_ _ _____

20_ _ _____

20_ _ _____

may 8

20__ _____

_____

_____

_____

_____

_____

20__ _____

_____

_____

_____

_____

_____

20__ _____

_____

_____

_____

_____

_____

may 9

20_ _ _____

_____

_____

_____

_____

20_ _ _____

_____

_____

_____

_____

20_ _ _____

_____

_____

_____

_____

may 10

20__ ————————————————————————

—————————————————————————————————

—————————————————————————————————

—————————————————————————————————

—————————————————————————————————

—————————————————————————————————

20__ ————————————————————————

—————————————————————————————————

—————————————————————————————————

—————————————————————————————————

—————————————————————————————————

—————————————————————————————————

20__ ————————————————————————

—————————————————————————————————

—————————————————————————————————

—————————————————————————————————

—————————————————————————————————

—————————————————————————————————

may 11

20_ _ _____

_____

_____

_____

_____

_____

20_ _ _____

_____

_____

_____

_____

_____

20_ _ _____

_____

_____

_____

_____

_____

^{may} 12

20___

20___

20___

Joy manifests itself
in the body.

^{may} 13

20_ _

20_ _

20_ _

20_ _ _____
_____
_____
_____
_____
_____

20_ _ _____
_____
_____
_____
_____
_____

20_ _ _____
_____
_____
_____
_____
_____

may 15

Does it spark joy?

20_ _ _____

_____

_____

_____

_____

_____

20_ _ _____

_____

_____

_____

_____

_____

20_ _ _____

_____

_____

_____

_____

_____

may 16

20_ _ _____

_____

_____

_____

_____

_____

20_ _ _____

_____

_____

_____

_____

_____

20_ _ _____

_____

_____

_____

_____

may 17

20_ _ _____

_____

_____

_____

_____

_____

20_ _ _____

_____

_____

_____

_____

_____

20_ _ _____

_____

_____

_____

_____

_____

20_ _ _____

_____

_____

_____

_____

20_ _ _____

_____

_____

_____

_____

20_ _ _____

_____

_____

_____

_____

may **19**

Does it spark joy?

20_ _ _____

_____

_____

_____

_____

20_ _ _____

_____

_____

_____

_____

20_ _ _____

_____

_____

_____

_____

may 20

20___ _____
_____
_____
_____
_____
_____

20___ _____
_____
_____
_____
_____
_____

20___ _____
_____
_____
_____
_____
_____

^{may} **21**

20_ _ _____

_____

_____

_____

_____

_____

20_ _ _____

_____

_____

_____

_____

_____

20_ _ _____

_____

_____

_____

_____

_____

may 22

20_ _ _____

_____

_____

_____

_____

20_ _ _____

_____

_____

_____

_____

20_ _ _____

_____

_____

_____

_____

may 23

Does it spark joy?

20_ _ _ _____

_____

_____

_____

_____

_____

20_ _ _ _____

_____

_____

_____

_____

_____

20_ _ _ _____

_____

_____

_____

_____

_____

may 24

20＿＿ _____
_____
_____
_____
_____
_____

20＿＿ _____
_____
_____
_____
_____

20＿＿ _____
_____
_____
_____
_____

Can you place your hand on your heart and swear that you are happy when surrounded by so much stuff that you don't even remember what's there?

^{may} **25**

20_ _ _____
_____
_____
_____
_____
_____

20_ _ _____
_____
_____
_____
_____
_____

20_ _ _____
_____
_____
_____
_____
_____

may 26

Does it spark joy?

20_ _ _____

_____

_____

_____

_____

_____

20_ _ _____

_____

_____

_____

_____

_____

20_ _ _____

_____

_____

_____

_____

_____

may 27

20_ _ _____

_____

_____

_____

_____

_____

20_ _ _____

_____

_____

_____

_____

20_ _ _____

_____

_____

_____

_____

^{may} 28

20_ _ _____

_____

_____

_____

_____

_____

20_ _ _____

_____

_____

_____

_____

_____

20_ _ _____

_____

_____

_____

_____

_____

may 29

20___ _____

_____

_____

_____

_____

20___ _____

_____

_____

_____

_____

20___ _____

_____

_____

_____

_____

may 30

Does it spark joy?

20___ _____

_____

_____

_____

_____

_____

20___ _____

_____

_____

_____

_____

_____

20___ _____

_____

_____

_____

_____

_____

may 31

20__ _____

_____

_____

_____

_____

20__ _____

_____

_____

_____

_____

20__ _____

_____

_____

_____

_____

june 1

20__ _____

_____

_____

_____

_____

_____

20__ _____

_____

_____

_____

_____

_____

20__ _____

_____

_____

_____

_____

_____

june 2

20_ _ _____

_____

_____

_____

_____

_____

20_ _ _____

_____

_____

_____

_____

_____

20_ _ _____

_____

_____

_____

_____

_____

june 3

Does it spark joy?

20__ _ _____

_____

_____

_____

_____

_____

20__ _ _____

_____

_____

_____

_____

_____

20__ _ _____

_____

_____

_____

_____

_____

june 4

20__ _____
_____
_____
_____
_____
_____

20__ _____
_____
_____
_____
_____
_____

20__ _____
_____
_____
_____
_____
_____

june 5

20___ _____

_____

_____

_____

_____

_____

20___ _____

_____

_____

_____

_____

_____

20___ _____

_____

_____

_____

_____

_____

Although not large, the
space I live in is graced
with only those things
that speak to my heart.
My lifestyle brings me joy.

june 6

20_ _ _____

_____

_____

_____

_____

20_ _ _____

_____

_____

_____

_____

20_ _ _____

_____

_____

_____

_____

june 7

20_ _ _____

_____

_____

_____

_____

20_ _ _____

_____

_____

_____

_____

20_ _ _____

_____

_____

_____

_____

june 8

20_ _ _____

_____

_____

_____

_____

_____

20_ _ _____

_____

_____

_____

_____

_____

20_ _ _____

_____

_____

_____

_____

_____

june 9

20_ _ _____

_____

_____

_____

_____

_____

20_ _ _____

_____

_____

_____

_____

_____

20_ _ _____

_____

_____

_____

_____

_____

june 10

20__ _____

_____

_____

_____

_____

_____

20__ _____

_____

_____

_____

_____

_____

20__ _____

_____

_____

_____

_____

_____

june 11

20__ _____

_____

_____

_____

_____

_____

20__ _____

_____

_____

_____

_____

_____

20__ _____

_____

_____

_____

_____

_____

Does it spark joy?

20_ _ _____

_____

_____

_____

_____

_____

20_ _ _____

_____

_____

_____

_____

_____

20_ _ _____

_____

_____

_____

_____

_____

june 13

20_ _ _____
_____
_____
_____
_____
_____

20_ _ _____
_____
_____
_____
_____
_____

20_ _ _____
_____
_____
_____
_____
_____

june 14

20_ _ _____

_____

_____

_____

_____

_____

20_ _ _____

_____

_____

_____

_____

_____

20_ _ _____

_____

_____

_____

_____

_____

june 15

20_ _ _____

_____

_____

_____

_____

_____

20_ _ _____

_____

_____

_____

_____

20_ _ _____

_____

_____

_____

_____

june **16**

Does it spark joy?

20____ _____

_____

_____

_____

_____

_____

20____ _____

_____

_____

_____

_____

_____

20____ _____

_____

_____

_____

_____

_____

june 17

20_ _ _____

_____

_____

_____

_____

_____

20_ _ _____

_____

_____

_____

_____

_____

20_ _ _____

_____

_____

_____

_____

_____

Look more closely
at what is there.

june 18

20_ _ _____

_____

_____

_____

_____

20_ _ _____

_____

_____

_____

_____

20_ _ _____

_____

_____

_____

_____

Does it spark joy?

20_ _

_____

_____

_____

_____

_____

20_ _

_____

_____

_____

_____

_____

20_ _

_____

_____

_____

_____

_____

june 20

20__ _____

_____

_____

_____

_____

_____

20__ _____

_____

_____

_____

_____

_____

20__ _____

_____

_____

_____

_____

_____

june 21

20_ _ _____

_____

_____

_____

_____

20_ _ _____

_____

_____

_____

_____

20_ _ _____

_____

_____

_____

_____

june 22

20_ _ _____

_____

_____

_____

_____

_____

20_ _ _____

_____

_____

_____

_____

_____

20_ _ _____

_____

_____

_____

_____

_____

june 23

Does it spark joy?

20_ _ —————————————————————————

———————————————————————————————

———————————————————————————————

———————————————————————————————

———————————————————————————————

———————————————————————————————

20_ _ —————————————————————————

———————————————————————————————

———————————————————————————————

———————————————————————————————

———————————————————————————————

———————————————————————————————

20_ _ —————————————————————————

———————————————————————————————

———————————————————————————————

———————————————————————————————

———————————————————————————————

———————————————————————————————

june 24

20__ _____

_____

_____

_____

_____

20__ _____

_____

_____

_____

_____

20__ _____

_____

_____

_____

_____

june 25

20_ _ _____

_____

_____

_____

_____

_____

20_ _ _____

_____

_____

_____

_____

_____

20_ _ _____

_____

_____

_____

_____

_____

june 26

20_ _ _____
_____
_____
_____
_____
_____

20_ _ _____
_____
_____
_____
_____
_____

20_ _ _____
_____
_____
_____
_____
_____

june **27**

Does it spark joy?

20_ _ _____

20_ _ _____

20_ _ _____

june 28

20__ _____

_____

_____

_____

_____

_____

20__ _____

_____

_____

_____

_____

_____

20__ _____

_____

_____

_____

_____

_____

june 29

20_ _ _____

_____

_____

_____

_____

20_ _ _____

_____

_____

_____

_____

20_ _ _____

_____

_____

_____

_____

Imagine yourself living in a space that contains only things that spark joy.

june 30

20_ _

20_ _

20_ _

july 1

20__ _____

_____

_____

_____

_____

20__ _____

_____

_____

_____

_____

20__ _____

_____

_____

_____

_____

july 2

20_ _ _____

_____

_____

_____

_____

20_ _ _____

_____

_____

_____

_____

20_ _ _____

_____

_____

_____

_____

july 3

20__ _____
_____
_____
_____
_____
_____

20__ _____
_____
_____
_____
_____
_____

20__ _____
_____
_____
_____
_____
_____

july 4

20_ _ _____

20_ _ _____

20_ _ _____

july 5

20_ _ _____

_____

_____

_____

_____

_____

20_ _ _____

_____

_____

_____

_____

_____

20_ _ _____

_____

_____

_____

_____

_____

july 6

Does it spark joy?

20＿＿

20＿＿

20＿＿

july 7

20_ _ _____

_____

_____

_____

_____

_____

20_ _ _____

_____

_____

_____

_____

_____

20_ _ _____

_____

_____

_____

_____

_____

july 8

20_ _ _____

_____

_____

_____

_____

_____

20_ _ _____

_____

_____

_____

_____

_____

20_ _ _____

_____

_____

_____

_____

_____

july 9

20_ _ _____

_____

_____

_____

_____

_____

20_ _ _____

_____

_____

_____

_____

_____

20_ _ _____

_____

_____

_____

_____

_____

Does it spark joy?

20_ _ _____

_____

_____

_____

_____

_____

20_ _ _____

_____

_____

_____

_____

_____

20_ _ _____

_____

_____

_____

_____

_____

july **11**

20_ _ _____

_____

_____

_____

_____

_____

20_ _ _____

_____

_____

_____

_____

_____

20_ _ _____

_____

_____

_____

_____

_____

Only you can know what kind of environment makes you feel happy.

july 12

20_ _ _____

_____

_____

_____

_____

20_ _ _____

_____

_____

_____

_____

20_ _ _____

_____

_____

_____

_____

july 13

20_ _ _____

_____

_____

_____

_____

_____

20_ _ _____

_____

_____

_____

_____

_____

20_ _ _____

_____

_____

_____

_____

_____

july 14

20_ _ _____

_____

_____

_____

_____

_____

20_ _ _____

_____

_____

_____

_____

_____

20_ _ _____

_____

_____

_____

_____

_____

july **15**

20_ _ _____

_____

_____

_____

_____

_____

20_ _ _____

_____

_____

_____

_____

_____

20_ _ _____

_____

_____

_____

_____

_____

july 16

20_ _ _____
_____
_____
_____
_____
_____

20_ _ _____
_____
_____
_____
_____
_____

20_ _ _____
_____
_____
_____
_____
_____

july 17

Does it spark joy?

20__ _____

_____

_____

_____

_____

_____

20__ _____

_____

_____

_____

_____

_____

20__ _____

_____

_____

_____

_____

_____

july 18

20__ _____
_____
_____
_____
_____
_____

20__ _____
_____
_____
_____
_____
_____

20__ _____
_____
_____
_____
_____
_____

july 19

20__ _____

_____

_____

_____

_____

_____

20__ _____

_____

_____

_____

_____

20__ _____

_____

_____

_____

_____

july 20

20__ _____
_____
_____
_____
_____
_____

20__ _____
_____
_____
_____
_____
_____

20__ _____
_____
_____
_____
_____
_____

july 21

Does it spark joy?

20_ _

_____

_____

_____

_____

_____

20_ _

_____

_____

_____

_____

_____

20_ _

_____

_____

_____

_____

_____

july 22

20_ _ _____

_____

_____

_____

_____

_____

20_ _ _____

_____

_____

_____

_____

_____

20_ _ _____

_____

_____

_____

_____

_____

july 23

20___ _____

20___ _____

20___ _____

Through the process of selecting only those things that inspire joy, you can identify precisely what you love and what you need.

july 24

20_ _ _____

_____

_____

_____

_____

20_ _ _____

_____

_____

_____

_____

20_ _ _____

_____

_____

_____

_____

july 25

20_ _ _____
_____
_____
_____
_____
_____

20_ _ _____
_____
_____
_____
_____
_____

20_ _ _____
_____
_____
_____
_____
_____

july **26**

20___ _____

_____

_____

_____

_____

_____

20___ _____

_____

_____

_____

_____

_____

20___ _____

_____

_____

_____

_____

_____

july 27

20＿＿ _____

_____

_____

_____

_____

_____

20＿＿ _____

_____

_____

_____

_____

_____

20＿＿ _____

_____

_____

_____

_____

_____

july 28

20__ _____

_____

_____

_____

_____

_____

20__ _____

_____

_____

_____

_____

_____

20__ _____

_____

_____

_____

_____

_____

july 29

20_ _ _____

_____

_____

_____

_____

_____

20_ _ _____

_____

_____

_____

_____

_____

20_ _ _____

_____

_____

_____

_____

_____

july 30

Does it spark joy?

20_ _ _____

_____

_____

_____

_____

20_ _ _____

_____

_____

_____

_____

20_ _ _____

_____

_____

_____

_____

july 31

20_ _ _____

_____

_____

_____

_____

_____

20_ _ _____

_____

_____

_____

_____

_____

20_ _ _____

_____

_____

_____

_____

_____

august 1

20＿＿ _____

_____

_____

_____

_____

_____

20＿＿ _____

_____

_____

_____

_____

_____

20＿＿ _____

_____

_____

_____

_____

_____

august 2

20_ _

20_ _

20_ _

august 3

Does it spark joy?

20_ _ _____

_____

_____

_____

_____

20_ _ _____

_____

_____

_____

_____

20_ _ _____

_____

_____

_____

_____

august 4

20__ _____

_____

_____

_____

_____

_____

20__ _____

_____

_____

_____

_____

_____

20__ _____

_____

_____

_____

_____

_____

Everyone needs a sanctuary.

august 5

20_ _ _____

_____

_____

_____

_____

_____

20_ _ _____

_____

_____

_____

_____

_____

20_ _ _____

_____

_____

_____

_____

_____

august 6

Does it spark joy?

20_ _ _____

_____

_____

_____

_____

20_ _ _____

_____

_____

_____

_____

20_ _ _____

_____

_____

_____

_____

august 7

20_ _ _____

_____

_____

_____

_____

_____

20_ _ _____

_____

_____

_____

_____

_____

20_ _ _____

_____

_____

_____

_____

_____

august 8

20_ _

20_ _

20_ _

august 9

20_ _ _____

_____

_____

_____

_____

20_ _ _____

_____

_____

_____

_____

20_ _ _____

_____

_____

_____

_____

august 10

Does it spark joy?

20_ _ _____

_____

_____

_____

_____

_____

20_ _ _____

_____

_____

_____

_____

_____

20_ _ _____

_____

_____

_____

_____

_____

august 11

20__ _____

_____

_____

_____

_____

_____

20__ _____

_____

_____

_____

_____

_____

20__ _____

_____

_____

_____

_____

_____

august 12

20__ _____

_____

_____

_____

_____

_____

20__ _____

_____

_____

_____

_____

_____

20__ _____

_____

_____

_____

_____

_____

august 13

20__ _____

_____

_____

_____

_____

_____

20__ _____

_____

_____

_____

_____

_____

20__ _____

_____

_____

_____

_____

_____

august 14

Does it spark joy?

20__ _____

_____

_____

_____

_____

_____

20__ _____

_____

_____

_____

_____

_____

20__ _____

_____

_____

_____

_____

_____

august 15

20_ _ _____

_____

_____

_____

_____

_____

20_ _ _____

_____

_____

_____

_____

_____

20_ _ _____

_____

_____

_____

_____

_____

august 16

20_ _ _____

_____

_____

_____

_____

_____

20_ _ _____

_____

_____

_____

_____

_____

20_ _ _____

_____

_____

_____

_____

_____

When we really delve
into the reasons for why
we can't let something
go, there are only two:
an attachment to the past
or a fear for the future.

august 17

20＿＿

20＿＿

20＿＿

august 18

20__ __ _____
_____
_____
_____
_____
_____

20__ __ _____
_____
_____
_____
_____
_____

20__ __ _____
_____
_____
_____
_____
_____

august 19

Does it spark joy?

20_ _ _____

20_ _ _____

20_ _ _____

august 20

20_ _ _ ———————————————————————

20_ _ _ ———————————————————————

20_ _ _ ———————————————————————

august 21

20__ _____
_____
_____
_____
_____
_____

20__ _____
_____
_____
_____
_____
_____

20__ _____
_____
_____
_____
_____
_____

august 22

20_ _ _____

_____

_____

_____

_____

_____

20_ _ _____

_____

_____

_____

_____

_____

20_ _ _____

_____

_____

_____

_____

_____

august 23

Does it spark joy?

20_ _ _____

_____

_____

_____

_____

_____

20_ _ _____

_____

_____

_____

_____

_____

20_ _ _____

_____

_____

_____

_____

_____

august 24

20__ _ _____

20__ _ _____

20__ _ _____

august 25

20_ _ _ —————————————————————————
—————————————————————————————
—————————————————————————————
—————————————————————————————
—————————————————————————————
—————————————————————————————

20_ _ _ —————————————————————————
—————————————————————————————
—————————————————————————————
—————————————————————————————
—————————————————————————————
—————————————————————————————

20_ _ _ —————————————————————————
—————————————————————————————
—————————————————————————————
—————————————————————————————
—————————————————————————————
—————————————————————————————

august 26

20_ _ _____

_____

_____

_____

_____

_____

20_ _ _____

_____

_____

_____

_____

_____

20_ _ _____

_____

_____

_____

_____

_____

august 27

Does it spark joy?

20_ _ _____

_____

_____

_____

_____

20_ _ _____

_____

_____

_____

_____

20_ _ _____

_____

_____

_____

_____

august 28

20＿＿ _____

_____

_____

_____

_____

_____

20＿＿ _____

_____

_____

_____

_____

_____

20＿＿ _____

_____

_____

_____

_____

_____

Attachment to the past and fears concerning the future not only govern the way you select the things you own but also represent the criteria by which you make choices in every aspect of your life, including your relationships with people and your job.

august **29**

20_ _ _____

_____

_____

_____

_____

_____

20_ _ _____

_____

_____

_____

_____

_____

20_ _ _____

_____

_____

_____

_____

_____

august **30**

20_ _ ———————————————————————————

—————————————————————————————————

—————————————————————————————————

—————————————————————————————————

—————————————————————————————————

—————————————————————————————————

20_ _ ———————————————————————————

—————————————————————————————————

—————————————————————————————————

—————————————————————————————————

—————————————————————————————————

—————————————————————————————————

20_ _ ———————————————————————————

—————————————————————————————————

—————————————————————————————————

—————————————————————————————————

—————————————————————————————————

—————————————————————————————————

august 31

20__ _____

_____

_____

_____

_____

_____

20__ _____

_____

_____

_____

_____

_____

20__ _____

_____

_____

_____

_____

_____

september 1

20＿＿

20＿＿

20＿＿

september 2

20_ _ _____

_____

_____

_____

_____

_____

20_ _ _____

_____

_____

_____

_____

_____

20_ _ _____

_____

_____

_____

_____

_____

september 3

Does it spark joy?

20_ _ _____
_____
_____
_____
_____

20_ _ _____
_____
_____
_____
_____

20_ _ _____
_____
_____
_____
_____

september 4

20___

20___

20___

september 5

20_ _ _____

_____

_____

_____

_____

_____

20_ _ _____

_____

_____

_____

_____

_____

20_ _ _____

_____

_____

_____

_____

_____

september 6

20_ _ _____

_____

_____

_____

_____

_____

20_ _ _____

_____

_____

_____

_____

_____

20_ _ _____

_____

_____

_____

_____

_____

september 7

Does it spark joy?

20_ _ _____

_____

_____

_____

_____

_____

20_ _ _____

_____

_____

_____

_____

_____

20_ _ _____

_____

_____

_____

_____

_____

september 8

20_ _ _____

_____

_____

_____

_____

_____

20_ _ _____

_____

_____

_____

_____

_____

20_ _ _____

_____

_____

_____

_____

_____

september 9

20_ _ _____

_____

_____

_____

_____

_____

20_ _ _____

_____

_____

_____

_____

_____

20_ _ _____

_____

_____

_____

_____

_____

Things that are cherished shine.

september 10

20_ _ _____

_____

_____

_____

_____

_____

20_ _ _____

_____

_____

_____

_____

_____

20_ _ _____

_____

_____

_____

_____

_____

september 11

20_ _ _____

_____

_____

_____

_____

_____

20_ _ _____

_____

_____

_____

_____

_____

20_ _ _____

_____

_____

_____

_____

_____

september 12

Does it spark joy?

20_ _ _____

_____

_____

_____

_____

20_ _ _____

_____

_____

_____

_____

20_ _ _____

_____

_____

_____

_____

september 13

20_ _ _____

_____

_____

_____

_____

_____

20_ _ _____

_____

_____

_____

_____

_____

20_ _ _____

_____

_____

_____

_____

_____

september 14

20_ _ _____

_____

_____

_____

_____

_____

20_ _ _____

_____

_____

_____

_____

_____

20_ _ _____

_____

_____

_____

_____

_____

september 15

20_ _ _____

_____

_____

_____

_____

_____

20_ _ _____

_____

_____

_____

_____

_____

20_ _ _____

_____

_____

_____

_____

_____

september 16

Does it spark joy?

20__ _____

_____

_____

_____

_____

_____

20__ _____

_____

_____

_____

_____

_____

20__ _____

_____

_____

_____

_____

_____

september 17

20_ _ _____
_____
_____
_____
_____
_____

20_ _ _____
_____
_____
_____
_____
_____

20_ _ _____
_____
_____
_____
_____
_____

september 18

20_ _ _____

20_ _ _____

20_ _ _____

september 19

20_ _ _____

_____

_____

_____

_____

20_ _ _____

_____

_____

_____

_____

20_ _ _____

_____

_____

_____

_____

september 20

Does it spark joy?

20_ _ _____

_____

_____

_____

_____

20_ _ _____

_____

_____

_____

_____

20_ _ _____

_____

_____

_____

_____

september 21

20_ _ _____

_____

_____

_____

_____

_____

20_ _ _____

_____

_____

_____

_____

_____

20_ _ _____

_____

_____

_____

_____

_____

Life becomes far easier
once you know that things
will still work out even if
you are lacking something.

september 22

20_ _ _____

_____

_____

_____

_____

_____

20_ _ _____

_____

_____

_____

_____

_____

20_ _ _____

_____

_____

_____

_____

_____

september 23

Does it spark joy?

20___ _____

_____

_____

_____

_____

20___ _____

_____

_____

_____

_____

20___ _____

_____

_____

_____

_____

september 24

20_ _ _____

_____

_____

_____

_____

_____

20_ _ _____

_____

_____

_____

_____

_____

20_ _ _____

_____

_____

_____

_____

_____

september 25

20_ _ _____

_____

_____

_____

_____

20_ _ _____

_____

_____

_____

_____

20_ _ _____

_____

_____

_____

_____

september 26

20_ _ _____

_____

_____

_____

_____

_____

20_ _ _____

_____

_____

_____

_____

_____

20_ _ _____

_____

_____

_____

_____

_____

september 27

Does it spark joy?

20_ _ _____

_____

_____

_____

_____

_____

20_ _ _____

_____

_____

_____

_____

_____

20_ _ _____

_____

_____

_____

_____

_____

september 28

20_ _ _____

_____

_____

_____

_____

_____

20_ _ _____

_____

_____

_____

_____

_____

20_ _ _____

_____

_____

_____

_____

_____

september 29

20_ _ _____
_____
_____
_____
_____
_____

20_ _ _____
_____
_____
_____
_____
_____

20_ _ _____
_____
_____
_____
_____
_____

september 30

20_ _ _____

20_ _ _____

20_ _ _____

october 1

Does it spark joy?

20_ _ _____

_____

_____

_____

_____

_____

20_ _ _____

_____

_____

_____

_____

_____

20_ _ _____

_____

_____

_____

_____

_____

october 2

20_ _ _____

_____

_____

_____

_____

_____

20_ _ _____

_____

_____

_____

_____

_____

20_ _ _____

_____

_____

_____

_____

_____

october 3

20_ _ _____

_____

_____

_____

_____

_____

20_ _ _____

_____

_____

_____

_____

_____

20_ _ _____

_____

_____

_____

_____

_____

The best way to find out what we really need is to get rid of what we don't.

october 4

20__ _____

_____

_____

_____

_____

_____

20__ _____

_____

_____

_____

_____

_____

20__ _____

_____

_____

_____

_____

_____

october 5

20___ _____

20___ _____

20___ _____

october 6

Does it spark joy?

20＿＿ _____

_____

_____

_____

_____

20＿＿ _____

_____

_____

_____

_____

20＿＿ _____

_____

_____

_____

_____

october 7

20__ _____

_____

_____

_____

_____

_____

20__ _____

_____

_____

_____

_____

_____

20__ _____

_____

_____

_____

_____

_____

october 8

20__

20__

20__

october 9

20_ _ _____

_____

_____

_____

_____

20_ _ _____

_____

_____

_____

_____

20_ _ _____

_____

_____

_____

_____

october 10

Does it spark joy?

20___

_____

_____

_____

_____

_____

20___

_____

_____

_____

_____

_____

20___

_____

_____

_____

_____

_____

october 11

20_ _ _____

_____

_____

_____

_____

_____

20_ _ _____

_____

_____

_____

_____

_____

20_ _ _____

_____

_____

_____

_____

_____

october 12

20_ _ _____

_____

_____

_____

_____

_____

20_ _ _____

_____

_____

_____

_____

_____

20_ _ _____

_____

_____

_____

_____

_____

october 13

20_ _ _____

_____

_____

_____

_____

_____

20_ _ _____

_____

_____

_____

_____

_____

20_ _ _____

_____

_____

_____

_____

_____

october 14

Does it spark joy?

20＿＿ _____

_____

_____

_____

_____

_____

20＿＿ _____

_____

_____

_____

_____

_____

20＿＿ _____

_____

_____

_____

_____

_____

october 15

20___ _____

_____

_____

_____

_____

_____

20___ _____

_____

_____

_____

_____

_____

20___ _____

_____

_____

_____

_____

Everyone has things that they love, things that they cannot imagine parting with, even though other people shake their heads in disbelief when they see them.

october 16

20＿＿ _____
_____
_____
_____
_____
_____

20＿＿ _____
_____
_____
_____
_____
_____

20＿＿ _____
_____
_____
_____
_____
_____

october **17**

Does it spark joy?

20_ _ _____

_____

_____

_____

_____

20_ _ _____

_____

_____

_____

_____

20_ _ _____

_____

_____

_____

_____

october 18

20_ _ _____

_____

_____

_____

_____

_____

20_ _ _____

_____

_____

_____

_____

_____

20_ _ _____

_____

_____

_____

_____

_____

october 19

20_ _ _____

20_ _ _____

20_ _ _____

october 20

20_ _ _____
_____
_____
_____
_____

20_ _ _____
_____
_____
_____
_____

20_ _ _____
_____
_____
_____
_____

october 21

Does it spark joy?

20_ _ _____

20_ _ _____

20_ _ _____

october 22

20_ _ _____

_____

_____

_____

_____

_____

20_ _ _____

_____

_____

_____

_____

_____

20_ _ _____

_____

_____

_____

_____

_____

october 23

20__ _____

_____

_____

_____

_____

_____

20__ _____

_____

_____

_____

_____

_____

20__ _____

_____

_____

_____

_____

_____

october 24

20_ _ _____

_____

_____

_____

_____

20_ _ _____

_____

_____

_____

_____

20_ _ _____

_____

_____

_____

_____

october 25

Does it spark joy?

20_ _ _____

_____

_____

_____

_____

20_ _ _____

_____

_____

_____

_____

20_ _ _____

_____

_____

_____

_____

october 26

20___ _ _____

20___ _ _____

20___ _ _____

october 27

20＿＿ _____

_____

_____

_____

_____

_____

20＿＿ _____

_____

_____

_____

_____

_____

20＿＿ _____

_____

_____

_____

_____

_____

I can think of no greater
happiness in life than to
be surrounded only by the
things I love.

october 28

20__ _____

20__ _____

20__ _____

october 29

20_ _ _____

_____

_____

_____

_____

_____

20_ _ _____

_____

_____

_____

_____

_____

20_ _ _____

_____

_____

_____

_____

_____

october 30

Does it spark joy?

20_ _ _____

_____

_____

_____

_____

_____

20_ _ _____

_____

_____

_____

_____

_____

20_ _ _____

_____

_____

_____

_____

_____

october **31**

20_ _ _____

_____

_____

_____

_____

20_ _ _____

_____

_____

_____

_____

20_ _ _____

_____

_____

_____

_____

november 1

20_ _ _____

20_ _ _____

20_ _ _____

november 2

20_ _ _____

_____

_____

_____

_____

_____

20_ _ _____

_____

_____

_____

_____

_____

20_ _ _____

_____

_____

_____

_____

_____

november 3

20___ _____

_____

_____

_____

_____

_____

20___ _____

_____

_____

_____

_____

_____

20___ _____

_____

_____

_____

_____

_____

november 4

20_ _ _____

_____

_____

_____

_____

_____

20_ _ _____

_____

_____

_____

_____

_____

20_ _ _____

_____

_____

_____

_____

_____

november 5

20_ _ _____

_____

_____

_____

_____

_____

20_ _ _____

_____

_____

_____

_____

_____

20_ _ _____

_____

_____

_____

_____

_____

november 6

20_ _ _____

20_ _ _____

20_ _ _____

november 7

20___ _____

_____

_____

_____

_____

20___ _____

_____

_____

_____

_____

20___ _____

_____

_____

_____

_____

november 8

20_ _ _____

_____

_____

_____

_____

20_ _ _____

_____

_____

_____

_____

20_ _ _____

_____

_____

_____

_____

All you need to do is
get rid of anything that
doesn't touch your heart.
There is no simpler way
to contentment.

november 9

20_ _ _____

_____

_____

_____

_____

_____

20_ _ _____

_____

_____

_____

_____

_____

20_ _ _____

_____

_____

_____

_____

_____

november 10

Does it spark joy?

20_ _ _____

_____

_____

_____

_____

_____

20_ _ _____

_____

_____

_____

_____

_____

20_ _ _____

_____

_____

_____

_____

_____

november 11

20_ _ _____

_____

_____

_____

_____

_____

20_ _ _____

_____

_____

_____

_____

_____

20_ _ _____

_____

_____

_____

_____

_____

november 12

20_ _ _____

20_ _ _____

20_ _ _____

november 13

20_ _ _____

_____

_____

_____

_____

_____

20_ _ _____

_____

_____

_____

_____

_____

20_ _ _____

_____

_____

_____

_____

_____

november 14

Does it spark joy?

20__ _____

_____

_____

_____

_____

20__ _____

_____

_____

_____

_____

20__ _____

_____

_____

_____

_____

november 15

20_ _ _____

_____

_____

_____

_____

_____

20_ _ _____

_____

_____

_____

_____

_____

20_ _ _____

_____

_____

_____

_____

_____

november 16

20_ _ _____
_____
_____
_____
_____
_____

20_ _ _____
_____
_____
_____
_____

20_ _ _____
_____
_____
_____
_____

november 17

20_ _ _____

_____

_____

_____

_____

_____

20_ _ _____

_____

_____

_____

_____

_____

20_ _ _____

_____

_____

_____

_____

_____

november 18

Does it spark joy?

20_ _ _____

_____

_____

_____

_____

_____

20_ _ _____

_____

_____

_____

_____

_____

20_ _ _____

_____

_____

_____

_____

_____

november 19

20_ _ _____
_____
_____
_____
_____
_____

20_ _ _____
_____
_____
_____
_____
_____

20_ _ _____
_____
_____
_____
_____
_____

november 20

20_ _ _____

_____

_____

_____

_____

20_ _ _____

_____

_____

_____

_____

20_ _ _____

_____

_____

_____

_____

Human beings can only
truly cherish a limited
number of things at
one time.

november 21

20_ _ _____

_____

_____

_____

_____

_____

20_ _ _____

_____

_____

_____

_____

_____

20_ _ _____

_____

_____

_____

_____

_____

november 22

20__ _____

_____

_____

_____

_____

20__ _____

_____

_____

_____

_____

20__ _____

_____

_____

_____

_____

november 23

Does it spark joy?

20_ _ _____

_____

_____

_____

_____

20_ _ _____

_____

_____

_____

_____

20_ _ _____

_____

_____

_____

_____

november 24

20＿＿ _____

_____

_____

_____

_____

_____

20＿＿ _____

_____

_____

_____

_____

20＿＿ _____

_____

_____

_____

_____

november 25

20_ _ _____

_____

_____

_____

_____

20_ _ _____

_____

_____

_____

_____

20_ _ _____

_____

_____

_____

_____

november 26

20_ _ _____

20_ _ _____

20_ _ _____

november 27

Does it spark joy?

20__ _____

_____

_____

_____

_____

_____

20__ _____

_____

_____

_____

_____

_____

20__ _____

_____

_____

_____

_____

_____

november 28

20_ _ _____

_____

_____

_____

_____

_____

20_ _ _____

_____

_____

_____

_____

20_ _ _____

_____

_____

_____

_____

_____

november 29

20__ _____

_____

_____

_____

_____

_____

20__ _____

_____

_____

_____

_____

_____

20__ _____

_____

_____

_____

_____

_____

november 30

20_ _ _____

_____

_____

_____

_____

_____

20_ _ _____

_____

_____

_____

_____

20_ _ _____

_____

_____

_____

_____

december 1

Does it spark joy?

20_ _ _____

_____

_____

_____

_____

_____

20_ _ _____

_____

_____

_____

_____

_____

20_ _ _____

_____

_____

_____

_____

_____

december 2

20_ _ _____

_____

_____

_____

_____

_____

20_ _ _____

_____

_____

_____

_____

_____

20_ _ _____

_____

_____

_____

_____

_____

I want to properly cherish
the things I love.

december 3

20_ _ _____

_____

_____

_____

_____

20_ _ _____

_____

_____

_____

_____

20_ _ _____

_____

_____

_____

_____

december 4

20_ _ _____

_____

_____

_____

_____

20_ _ _____

_____

_____

_____

_____

20_ _ _____

_____

_____

_____

_____

december 5

20__ _____
_____
_____
_____
_____
_____

20__ _____
_____
_____
_____
_____
_____

20__ _____
_____
_____
_____
_____
_____

december 6

20_ _ _____

_____

_____

_____

_____

_____

20_ _ _____

_____

_____

_____

_____

_____

20_ _ _____

_____

_____

_____

_____

_____

december 7

20__ _____
_____
_____
_____
_____
_____

20__ _____
_____
_____
_____
_____
_____

20__ _____
_____
_____
_____
_____
_____

december 8

Does it spark joy?

20_ _ _____

_____

_____

_____

_____

20_ _ _____

_____

_____

_____

_____

20_ _ _____

_____

_____

_____

_____

december 9

20_ _ _____

_____

_____

_____

_____

20_ _ _____

_____

_____

_____

_____

20_ _ _____

_____

_____

_____

_____

december 10

20__ _____

_____

_____

_____

_____

_____

20__ _____

_____

_____

_____

_____

_____

20__ _____

_____

_____

_____

_____

_____

december 11

20_ _ _____

_____

_____

_____

_____

_____

20_ _ _____

_____

_____

_____

_____

_____

20_ _ _____

_____

_____

_____

_____

_____

december 12

Does it spark joy?

20_ _ _____

_____

_____

_____

_____

_____

20_ _ _____

_____

_____

_____

_____

_____

20_ _ _____

_____

_____

_____

_____

_____

The things and people that bring me joy support me. They give me the confidence that I will be all right.

december 13

20_ _ _____

_____

_____

_____

_____

_____

20_ _ _____

_____

_____

_____

_____

_____

20_ _ _____

_____

_____

_____

_____

_____

december 14

20_ _ _____

_____
_____
_____
_____
_____

20_ _ _____

_____
_____
_____
_____
_____

20_ _ _____

_____
_____
_____
_____
_____

december 15

Does it spark joy?

20_ _ _____

_____

_____

_____

_____

20_ _ _____

_____

_____

_____

_____

20_ _ _____

_____

_____

_____

_____

december 16

20___ _____

_____

_____

_____

_____

20___ _____

_____

_____

_____

_____

20___ _____

_____

_____

_____

_____

december 17

20_ _ _____

_____

_____

_____

_____

_____

20_ _ _____

_____

_____

_____

_____

_____

20_ _ _____

_____

_____

_____

_____

_____

december 18

20___ _____

20___ _____

20___ _____

december 19

Does it spark joy?

20_ _

20_ _

20_ _

december 20

20＿＿ _____

_____

_____

_____

_____

_____

20＿＿ _____

_____

_____

_____

_____

_____

20＿＿ _____

_____

_____

_____

_____

_____

december 21

20___ _____

_____

_____

_____

_____

20___ _____

_____

_____

_____

_____

20___ _____

_____

_____

_____

_____

december 22

20_ _ _____

_____

_____

_____

_____

20_ _ _____

_____

_____

_____

_____

20_ _ _____

_____

_____

_____

_____

december 23

Does it spark joy?

20_ _ _____

_____

_____

_____

_____

_____

20_ _ _____

_____

_____

_____

_____

_____

20_ _ _____

_____

_____

_____

_____

_____

december 24

20_ _ _____

_____

_____

_____

_____

_____

20_ _ _____

_____

_____

_____

_____

_____

20_ _ _____

_____

_____

_____

_____

_____

When it comes to the things I own, the clothes I wear, the house I live in, and the people in my life, when it comes to my environment as a whole, although it may not seem particularly special to anyone else, I am confident and extremely grateful to be surrounded by what I love, by things and people that are, each and every one, special, precious, and exceedingly dear to me.

december 25

20__ _____

_____

_____

_____

_____

20__ _____

_____

_____

_____

_____

20__ _____

_____

_____

_____

_____

december 26

Does it spark joy?

20__ _ _____

_____

_____

_____

_____

20__ _ _____

_____

_____

_____

_____

20__ _ _____

_____

_____

_____

_____

december 27

20_ _ _____

20_ _ _____

20_ _ _____

december 28

20___ _____

20___ _____

20___ _____

december 29

20_ _ _____

_____

_____

_____

_____

20_ _ _____

_____

_____

_____

_____

20_ _ _____

_____

_____

_____

_____

december 30

20_ _ _____

_____

_____

_____

_____

_____

20_ _ _____

_____

_____

_____

_____

_____

20_ _ _____

_____

_____

_____

_____

_____

december 31

20_ _ _____

_____

_____

_____

_____

_____

20_ _ _____

_____

_____

_____

_____

_____

20_ _ _____

_____

_____

_____

_____

_____